SAY "YES"
TO GOLF WITH ANYONE

SAY "YES"
TO GOLF WITH ANYONE

A Woman Golfer's Guide to
Confidence and Etiquette

Tammy Jo Laurent
Co-Owner, Stonebrooke Golf Club

Paperback ISBN: 978-1-955541-04-6
LCCN: 2022901127

Cover and interior design by Ann Aubitz

First Printing: February 2022

First Edition

Published by FuzionPress
1250 E 115th Street
Burnsville, MN 55337
FuzionPress.com
612-781-2815

I dedicate this book to Gary, my spouse and favorite golfing partner.

TABLE OF CONTENTS

"I promised my ball it's going to
be happy this time."

INTRODUCTION

Why I'm Writing This Book

I think we've all heard the lyrics by Rod Stewart, "I wish that ... I knew what I know now ... when I was younger."

That exact feeling led me to write this book. I work in finance, a very male-dominated field. Doing a little work while playing golf with clients is common in my world. Years ago, I was feeling left out when colleagues would head to the golf course while I stayed behind. I was missing out on learning from others I worked with, tips from product partners and vendors, and information from people in the home office because I was reluctant to play with anyone other than my sisters.

It wasn't that they didn't ask me to join them, because they did. I had a tremendous fear of breaking the "rules" I had heard so much about, and I didn't want to look like I wasn't up to par. I finally realized that if I wanted to be included at work functions, I had to learn to be comfortable on the golf course.

Luck intervened. I began to date a man who built and owned a golf course. Now I had a whole new level of etiquette to be concerned about. I found that the best way around it was to confess my ignorance. "I don't know all the rules and etiquette, so if you don't mind, let me know if I'm doing something I shouldn't." My admission left the door open for him to nicely point out my shortcomings. I didn't have as much pressure to be perfect. We married a few years later, and today, we still enjoy playing a game of golf together, even though he's a long-time player and I'm not.

It took lessons and many rounds of golf to get to where I am today. My hope is that golfers who are new to the sport can read this book over a lunch break, then head to the course in the afternoon and feel comfortable. The rules of golf are complicated, and as most golfers know, there are many of them. Over time, I've seen golfers of all skill levels break a rule now and then, but étiquette is étiquette. If you don't follow it, you will probably annoy your fellow golfers. Trust me, when you know a few of these simple manners, you'll fit in beautifully and enjoy the game as much as any par golfer—that is, as much as a super good player.

Every future golfer thinks, "I've never golfed before, but I'd love to try." This book is not meant to encourage you to rush out to the course without ever having taken a lesson and never having hit some balls at a practice range. Golf is a learned skill, and it takes some time. This book is designed to help you feel comfortable golfing with anyone once you've learned the basic skills of the game.

This book is not an instructional book that will teach you to play in thirty minutes. I would highly recommend taking a few lessons to become somewhat comfortable swinging the club and hitting the ball before you make your way to the golf course. It's not a natural movement for most, and learning to hit the ball is more easily done on the driving range, not the golf course. Many driving ranges or practice ranges offer wonderful clinics for new golfers. There are also community education classes, or you can call the golf pro at most courses and take some private lessons.

Any option above will help, but one way or another, getting some practice beforehand is a *must* before heading to the course to play with anyone. I've run into people who have never played before who think that they will just go out and try it. That's not really how it works. You don't want to head to the course until you have spent some pretty serious time working on your swing at the range or in private lessons. That's the best way to "try it," and if you don't like it there, you're not going to like playing on the course either. Trust me, the people you are golfing with won't appreciate either if you haven't ever hit a ball before and decide today is the day.

In order to learn the etiquette of golf, you need to know a bit about the game. Don't be the person who shows up at the course never having really swung a club before who's pretty sure that just because she's athletic, she can figure it out. This book is about feeling comfortable playing with others at any level *after* you've put in the practice time. It's very common for the course to pair up you and your friend with another twosome, so you are often golfing with two people you've never met before. That used to be daunting and uncomfortable for me. Now, I look forward to meeting new people, learning things about those people and the game, and having a good time.

This book includes all the things I wish I had known before I started playing with colleagues, clients, and my future husband. I can only imagine what they were thinking about my play before I knew the rules and the accompanying etiquette.

An interesting thing about golf is that, in actuality, there are two sets of rules, one for the serious golfer and one for the casual weekend golfer. When I am playing with a bunch of men from work, I play by the serious rules (the USGA rules). When I am golfing with my sisters, we laugh and talk a lot. We definitely play by the casual-golfer rules. I will attempt to give you both sets of rules and explain when each applies.

I don't claim to be a great golfer, but I have fun with the game. The best parts for me are being outdoors and enjoying the company of others. I know that whoever golfs with me is going to enjoy their game as well. I take pride in making sure they're having a great day on the course, no matter what the scorecard says. Maybe some day, I'll get to golf with you too!

HOLE NUMBER 1

What to Wear?

I could have said Chapter 1, but Hole Number 1 is so much more fun.

There is no perfect answer. Courses differ as to dress codes. If you want to be very safe, follow this common rule: most courses require your shirt or sweater to have a collar and don't allow jeans, cutoffs, or denim in general, and some might even frown upon shorts. Check with the course about its particular dress code before arriving.

There isn't a specific reason for the attire and protocol. However, one can speculate that it is to maintain the sport's traditions. Many of them date back to Scotland where the roots of golf can be traced to 1457. In fact, a long-spread rumor is that golf actually stands for "Gentleman Only, Ladies Forbidden." This appears to be an old wives' tale that has made it into circulation, which, though interesting, is not a fact.

You'll find many variations on dress code. Many courses today allow shorts but require that the length comes to your knee. Others still don't allow shorts at all. Golf courses in Europe are very particular about attire. Some even require socks worn to your knee or that men wear pants. If you are planning to golf anywhere, domestic or international, be sure to inquire about the dress code. I'd hate for you to get to Europe only to find out that you shouldn't have left your black knee-high socks at home.

In my early days of golfing, I was invited by a salesperson to golf at the Hazeltine National Golf Club in Minnesota, which happens to be the course chosen for many PGA events and a recent Ryder Cup. When it comes to golf, it's as fancy as Minnesota gets. I wasn't much of a golfer but said yes. That was my first mistake. I went to the store the night before and bought a t-shirt that I thought was perfect because the graphic on the front was colorful golf tees that spelled out the word "golf." I was sure that I'd be right in style. The next day as we checked in at the clubhouse, there was a lot of discussion going on that I couldn't hear. Later, I found out that the course had not been happy with my choice of apparel because my shirt hadn't had a collar. They had been trying to tell my host that I needed to buy a shirt with a collar from their pro shop or I wouldn't be able golf. My host ended up convincing them to let it go. I didn't understand why my "golf" t-shirt was not appropriate, but it wasn't. It was simply a rule that I hadn't known at the time. In retrospect, I am embarrassed.

Looking back, I shake my head and wish I'd had a book like this before I even drove to the course. A little knowledge of golf etiquette goes a long way.

Rules on attire are more relaxed now. Most courses post them on their website; you can also call and ask them to explain their requirements. Some courses allow jeans—and even short shorts—which are sported by some of the golf greats these days. Wearing shorts, which used to be a huge "no-no," is now quite in vogue.

When picking your golf attire, keep in mind that you will be leaning over often to pick up your ball, bending over your ball when addressing it, et cetera. A little modesty will make you and the others in your foursome more comfortable. I prefer skorts (skirt-like shorts) with pockets so that I have a place to put my extra ball, tees, and ball marker.

"What shoes should I wear?" People now wear golf shoes that vary from the traditional saddle shoe to those designed like a running shoe. If you don't have golf shoes, don't sweat it. Regular tennis shoes or running shoes are almost as good, especially for beginners. There was a time when golf shoes traditionally had metal spikes, but that is now frowned upon. They are not allowed on most courses as they are tough on the greens and the clubhouse floor.

"Should I wear a glove?" My husband never wears one. I wear mine all the time. Some people remove the glove for putting. It is a matter of preference rather than a rule. Do whatever works for you. You wear the glove on your non-dominant hand, so a right-handed person would wear a glove on her left hand.

The original purpose of a glove was to cushion your hand from the very hard grip on clubs made before the 1920s, but most professionals did not wear one. Sam Snead was the first major golfer to wear a glove, and that was sometime in the 1930s.

Now most golfers wear one—because virtually all the pros do. It's part of the look. Its purpose is to create friction, to give you a stronger grip, and to prevent callouses. Most newer clubs, however, have such nice grips that a glove isn't totally necessary. You choose.

"Should I wear a hat?" Baseballs caps and all kinds of other hats and visors are very common. It is definitely personal preference whether you want a hat, sunglasses, or neither.

"I'll be right there, as soon as I finish this text."

HOLE NUMBER 2

Arriving at the Course

Allow plenty of time to get to the course, arriving at least thirty minutes before your tee time. Most courses actually prefer you to arrive thirty minutes early. You should be at the first tee five minutes before your actual tee time.

Golf courses keep very tight time schedules. In fact, if you arrive late, your foursome may have left without you, leaving you to catch up with them at Hole 2 or 3. If your entire foursome is late, you may have to completely skip the first hole or two to get back on track.

You need to arrive at the course early enough to get everything out of your car, organize your bag, put your keys and wallet away, apply sunscreen, get your sunglasses and glove on, and buy beverages, if you choose. Getting checked in at the front counter may also take a few minutes, and you may want time to use the restroom.

Give yourself enough time to relax and, ideally, to practice putting for five to ten minutes on the practice green before you head to the first tee. This will make you a better player—and will make it more fun. I enjoy the game more and tend to play better if I have had time to mentally slow down and prepare rather than come rushing in at the last minute.

Many golfers show up early enough to go to the driving range or practice range and hit a few balls before they head to the first tee. My only caution is not to hit one hundred balls in practice because you'll be worn out before you start. This is called "leaving your game on the practice range." Hitting a few balls with each club and putting for five minutes should be more than enough preparation.

Before taking time to practice, you will pay at the front counter. One person may reserve the tee time, but when everyone shows up, it is common for each player to pay his or her own way. When the beverage cart comes around, assume you're going to pay for your own but know that it's common for people to take turns and offer to pay for the others in the foursome. "Hey, do you want anything to drink?" The same rules apply on the course as when you are getting a drink at a bar. Take your turn paying. Don't be one of *those* people.

When I arrive at the first tee to play with people, particularly men, with whom I don't normally golf, I can sense their apprehension. They are most likely thinking back to the last bad round when they were paired with a woman. They fear I'm going to play too slow, talk too much, and possibly not know the rules. I have found the best thing to say as I approach the group, is, "Hey guys, even though I'm not the best golfer on the course, I can guarantee you two things. We're going to have fun, and we're going to play fast." I can almost see them exhale a sigh of relief, relax a bit, and get ready to have a great day of golf.

**"I wonder how far this seven iron will go....
when I throw it."**

HOLE NUMBER 3

Driving the Golf Cart

T here are three ways to get around the course: walk and carry your clubs, (which isn't very common), walk and bring your clubs on a push or pull cart (you can bring your own or rent one), or drive a cart that holds two people (rented from the course—unless you own your own). Some courses now offer Segways as another option. Numerous courses will not allow you to walk, for several reasons. It can slow down the pace of play, and sometimes there are very long distances between holes, making it unconducive to walking. If you want to walk, you will need to check with the course in advance and see if they allow it.

Many courses have a bag-drop area where you can unload your golf clubs and proceed to park the car. Some do not have a bag drop but will meet you at your car to help carry your clubs. At some courses, you carry your own clubs.

Note: For liability reasons, some courses do not allow their golf carts to be driven in the parking lot next to cars.

My recommendation: Don't offer to drive the cart if you've never driven or ridden in one before. You can practice driving on the last hole—after someone else has driven the rest of the day.

Starting the cart is easy. Turn the key to the start position. Then put the cart in drive. D to go forward and R for reverse. (Reverse makes a loud beeping noise, so use it sparingly.) Like the pedals in a car, the gas is on the right and the brake on the left. Some carts have a smaller pedal on the top of the brake pedal that you push down to lock the brake. However, some automatically lock once you've stopped with the brake. Many carts will even make a noise if you leave and have not locked the brake before leaving the cart. There's nothing more entertaining than watching a cart head for the lake while its driver is walking toward her ball. It's definitely more fun if it is someone else's cart, not yours.

Driving the cart can be a bit tricky. You will need to know the rules for the course on that day. The staff should tell you upon checking in, or the rules may be posted on the cart.

"Cart Path Only" means stay on the path at *all* times. This may be a permanent course rule or a temporary one following a recent rain. The only time you may venture off the path is to pass a cart that is in your way, as long as it doesn't mean that you are driving somewhere you shouldn't.

Example: One player has hit her drive to the far right. You have hit to the far left, and your drive is a shorter distance. They may drop you off at your ball. Take whichever clubs you think you might need. If you're not sure, take several. Don't waste time walking back and forth from the cart to the ball to get another club because you grabbed the wrong one. If you are close to the green, you may want to grab your wedge and putter and walk to the green while the other person drives the cart to the green.

Another example: Your partner has hit her drive to the far right again. You have hit to the far left. She hit her drive shorter. Usually, she would drive the cart to the shortest ball, then move on to her ball. You may choose to take a few clubs and walk to your ball—once again taking two to three clubs that you might use. All these tips are to keep a good pace-of-play, which I will explain more about later.

Never drive on the greens or apron or even close to them. Not Ever. (The greens are the well-manicured very-short grasses around the flag. The apron or fringe is the area surrounding the green.) Think of the greens (or green) as a small sacred spot of very sensitive grass.

Where to park the cart while progressing down the fairway is another issue. Park behind your golfing partner's intended line of flight and far enough away that she doesn't feel cramped and afraid to take a full swing. I like to ask the person I'm golfing with whether he or she has a preference as to where I park the cart. I also don't have a problem letting someone know where I like the cart. A few weeks ago, I was playing with a guy who kept parking the cart almost on the exact spot where I wanted to stand to hit the ball. Then I realized that he was a lefty. He was thinking about it from his point of view. We laughed about it, and he graciously agreed to park on the other side of the ball.

I also golfed with someone who kept pulling their cart ahead of where I hit my ball to where if did hit an errant shot, it could actually hit them. Not only that, but when I addressed the ball, I could see them sitting there looking at me, and it made me uncomfortable. I very nicely said, "Hey, I'm sorry to have to ask, but I'm wondering if you guys wouldn't mind parking a little behind my ball. It's just something I'm a little particular about."

It was that simple. Had I not said anything, it would have stressed me out every time they did it.

Drop your partner off at their ball and either wait for her to hit or go to yours and hit. She can either walk back to the cart or you can drive and pick her up. If you are being dropped off, always take a few different clubs to your ball. If you and your cart-mate's balls are relatively close to each other, park in between them. The person who is farthest from the hole hits her ball first.

It is also a good idea to drive your cart in slightly different paths than others have used so you don't start making a road where one was not intended. On some courses, they mark where on the paved path you can leave the path and drive onto the fairway, but I always try to drive where no one else does so as to not wear out the grass. Many people cut the corners on the cart paths and create dead spots of grass. It is best if you don't cut the corners.

Do not drive up to the next tee when the people ahead of you are still teeing off. Hold back. They don't need you as an audience. Give the group privacy—the same privacy you want when it's your turn to drive the ball. There will be people who pull their cart up to your tee and violate this rule, and I don't have a solution for this problem. My best advice is to get used to people watching you play. If I have a terrible drive, I love to say something like, "Well, I'm obviously standing too close to the ball . . . after I hit it." Or I smile and say, "Well I'm glad I got that one out of my system."

Unfortunately, not all people will have had the advantage of reading this book. I'm working on my own tolerance of distractions such as lawn mowers, maintenance workers, and other golfers. I use confident self-talk and say, "I can't wait to show this guy my awesome swing." And when it doesn't go exactly as planned, I shrug and move on, knowing it happens to everyone—even the pros on TV.

"She'd be a lot more fun to golf with if she golfed as fast as she talks."

HOLE NUMBER 4

Pace-of-Play

Much of the etiquette in golf has to do with the speed of play, which is called "pace-of-play." Golf is one of the few sports in which a novice player and an expert player can golf side by side at the same pace, can compete with themselves, and can both enjoy the game. This is not true in most sports, which makes golf one of the most versatile and fun games you can play. You can enjoy it with your husband, your grandmother, and your grandchild all at the same time as long as everyone maintains a good pace-of-play. Everyone will be challenged by the game and will enjoy the outdoors and the company.

Pace-of-play makes this possible. It is designed to make golf enjoyable for your foursome and the seventy-two or more golfers on the course behind you. If you do nothing else right, make sure you are not holding up pace-of-play.

How do you do that? First, let's talk about preparing for your shot. A pro takes eight seconds. You need to be doing everything you can before you take your shot. If you're teeing off, decide where you're going to stand, have your club, ball, and tee in your hand, and have an extra ball in your pocket.

From the time you select the club to actually hitting the ball, you should take no more than thirty to forty-five seconds. If your pre-shot routine is longer than that, try to shorten it. I once played with a woman who loved to take four to five practice shots before each actual hit, and then she would bob up and down like a bird so many times, I would wonder whether she was actually going to come up with a worm. She definitely needed a shorter routine.

The person farthest from the hole hits first. If you are at your ball, and it's not your turn to hit, feel free to take a few practice swings, but only if your swing isn't going to distract the person actually hitting the ball. Be ready when it is your turn.

The four of you should progress down the fairway at relatively the same speed; some taking more shots than others. Because I tend to hit the ball more than my husband, I try to make up a little time by getting to my next shot quickly and having a very-short pre-shot routine.

I played with a new group of women last year. Their pace of play was, well…not good. They followed all rules of pace-of-play except one. They had developed this odd habit of helping each other find their balls. They actually looked at me as though I was rude when I followed my own ball rather than following each of them to their balls. Their deviation from a more standard and efficient practice took several extra minutes on each hole. They all walked to each of the four balls together and waited for each person to hit, rather than simply walking to their own ball. In an attempt to be polite, they were actually annoying all the golfers behind them who were having a slow, slow day on the course—not getting home to their families when promised, or not being on time for their next commitment.

As golf-course owners, the biggest complaint we hear, and the hardest problem to remedy, is "slow play." If a course consistently plays too slow, a golfer may never come back to that course again. It's such a slippery slope because people also don't like being told to pick up their pace. Some courses have a ranger who rides around on a cart and makes sure people are keeping up with the four-some ahead of them. This may seem like a good idea, but slow players hate it. Fast people hate it too because they expect the ranger to work miracles. It is a serious problem because a slow golfer might be one of the course's best customers, with lots of friends who also play golf. When slow golfers are told to pick up their pace of play, they are not happy and may tell all their friends that they hate the course, even expressing their views on social media. It's possible they don't even know they are doing anything wrong. They may not know *how* to play faster, and they can cause big problems for the course owners and the rangers.

As you progress down the fairway, the strictest rules would say you should *never* walk or ride in front of someone else's ball. Everyone progresses roughly at the same pace, always progressing to the next ball. However, when I am with my sisters, we deviate from this at times.

If a person's ball is on the other side of the fairway and she thinks she might have to search a bit, she might proceed ahead to find her ball, even if someone else's ball is farther back.

You don't ever want to be standing in a spot that makes someone uncomfortable hitting her ball, worried she might hit you. If you accidentally end up in someone's way, just apologize and move out of her path. There are times when I can't remember where all four people hit their balls and accidentally drive past someone's ball to get to another. It happens. No big deal. Apologize—and don't make a habit of it.

Once you hit onto the green, move over to your ball while others are approaching the green with their balls. If you are following stricter rules, you will want to mark your ball. Place a marker (which you should already have in your pocket) down behind the ball so that it doesn't make a mark in the grass where you intend to putt. A marker is a small round object used to mark your ball. It may have a spike that you can push into the ground. If someone doesn't have a marker, they might just use a dime. If I'm playing with my sisters, we only mark our balls if one seems like it might be in someone's way.

If everyone is on the green and your ball is farthest out, place your ball down, pick up your marker, and putt. Whoever is farthest out putts next. Never ever step on the line of your playing partner. The line is the path between the ball and the cup (that is, the hole). If you are a beginner and take more than three putts, you may have the others in your group saying "that's in" or "that's good enough." They are simply trying to keep up pace-of-play. Pick up your ball and move on.

One fascinating difference I have found between golfing with men and golfing with women is that men tend to call a ball that is "within the leathers" (which means within the distance between the hole and the length of your club) "good enough"—meaning that you don't have to make the putt, you can simply pick up the ball and pretend you made the putt, taking only one stroke. (A stroke is a point in golf.) Whereas had you missed the putt, it would be two strokes. They will also call some close puts "within the circle of friendship," which just means that you're close enough, so don't bother putting it out. They will do this to be friendly but also to keep up good pace-of-play.

Women, on the other hand, very rarely give each other putts and tend to putt everything out. There's nothing wrong with that. It's just something I've noticed.

If everyone is standing around patiently waiting, it may be because it's your turn to hit. If you have to ask, "Am I out?" you probably are. The person with the ball farthest away from the hole putts first, and so on. Don't ask; be ready. Once the last ball farther from the hole than yours has started toward the cup, move to your ball and start your routine. Even if someone is off the green but closer to the hole, the person on the green and farthest from the hole goes first.

Try and line up your putt while others are putting. Make sure you are far enough away that you aren't distracting them. Like most people, I like everyone perfectly still on the green when I am lining up my putt. If someone is moving around, even if she is behind me a bit, my eye wants to follow her rather than the line of the putt.

Another good practice is to never stand directly behind the person putting.

As soon as all four in a group are done sinking their putts, drive the cart to the next hole to open up the green for the next group coming through. Try not to chat about the hole or add up and write down your score while you are still parked at the hole. I find that this is the biggest complaint men have about women golfers. Progress to the next hole, then write down scores, preferably when it's not your turn to hit.

Golfers go out in foursomes for a reason. The timing the course has allowed for each hole is based on that number. Don't *ever* try to talk them into letting you have a five-some. It simply doesn't work. It takes too much time, and honestly, the few times I have golfed in a five-some, I haven't enjoyed it as much. You end up waiting too long before hitting your ball.

Some non-golfers like to ride along in the cart, which is fine. The only exception to this practice is if a vendor is paying for everyone's round of golf, and someone in the company says, "I'm not a golfer, but I'll ride along." Just know that when this happens, the vendor typically still has to pay for that person, and it prevents someone else from being able to golf with the group.

A good rule of thumb for pace-of-play is that if you are immediately behind the foursome in front of you, you are doing well. If there is a gap between you and the foursome ahead of you, you are probably a little slow. Occasionally the group in front of you is a twosome and you are a foursome. You won't keep up with them. In general, a good rule of thumb is to make sure the group behind you is *never* waiting for you to advance. If they are waiting for you, you are probably too slow.

I have noticed that carts equipped with GPS will often show whether you are keeping pace or are ahead or behind. This is very helpful.

Here is a little trick you can use if your foursome is falling behind in pace-of-play. If the tee in front of you is open and you have finished putting, announce to your foursome that you are going to go tee off to speed up your pace of play. Leave your foursome, go to the next hole, and tee off. You are breaking etiquette by not standing there and watching everyone putt out, but sometimes it is a good choice.

Often, courses have an employee who drives around on a golf cart offering drinks and snacks from a beverage cart. If you are buying something, it's best if the others in your foursome keep advancing play while you treat. As in any situation, it is best if everyone takes a turn buying treats. Then the others can get theirs while you are hitting. This eliminates situations where all four people are standing around the beverage cart slowing down pace-of-play.

Many courses offer hot dogs or quick food at the turn. The *turn* is between Holes 9 and 10, which is considered halfway, since there are eighteen holes. This is

also a great time to make a quick restroom s
are often restrooms or Porta Potties on the cc
with their locations usually designated on th

Most courses allow the same time for the turn
they do for one par-four hole. So, if the course is allowing
ten minutes for a par-four, they are allowing ten minutes
for the turn. They are assuming you will NOT go in the
clubhouse, order a hamburger, and catch up with old
friends. You are still following the pace during the turn.

I am warning you: when you are a novice golfer,
keeping up with the foursome ahead of you can be a challenge. Even keeping up with the other three players in
your foursome will be hard at times. Here's what you do.
If you are falling behind, there is nothing wrong with
picking up your ball and playing it from somewhere farther up the hole. As a beginner, you should not fret over
trying to get a great score. It doesn't really matter. Everyone in your foursome will be much happier if you pick
your ball up once in a while before finishing the hole so
you aren't slowing them down. Particularly on the green,
if you need more than three or four putts, pick your ball
up and make everyone happy.

If you lose a few balls, let them go. When you are a
beginner, leave the expensive Pro V1 balls at home. If
looking for a lost ball is holding up play, stop. Just drop
another ball down. Always keep an extra ball in your
pocket, drop it, and hit. Don't be one of those people
that has to run back to the cart to get another ball, or

worse yet, has to borrow one from someone else. Yes, it happens to everyone once in a while, but don't make a habit of it.

"Ohmigawd, of course I want front row tickets to the concert tonight."

HOLE NUMBER 5

On the Tee Box

Before we hit the first ball, it is important to talk a bit about handicaps. As a beginning golfer, you may not have a handicap yet, but it is an index that allows golfers of all abilities to compete in a fair and equitable manner. If you are ever asked to play in a tournament, you will most likely be required to establish one. Your local club can help you, or you may go online and set up an account that will track your scores and ultimately create a handicap with as few as three rounds. If you ever play in Scotland or Ireland you may be required to have an established handicap before playing certain courses.

Many people play "honors," which means that whoever had the best score on the last hole is the first to drive on the next hole.

Often the casual golfer plays what we call "ready-golf." My sisters and I play ready-golf every Wednesday. This means that whoever is ready hits the ball. As I mentioned before, there are two sets of rules. If in doubt, play by the serious rules.

I recently golfed with the starter (the person who sees you off at the first tee) at our golf club. He had been a very serious golfer years ago, and I asked him to give me tips that might be helpful as I start golfing with clients and strangers. He said that before he tees off the first hole, he asks the rest of the people in his foursome, "Are we playing by USGA rules today, or are we just out here to have fun?" That sets the tone for which etiquette to follow.

The tee area uses several different colored markers to distinguish where you place your tee and ball. All courses differ on what colors they use. The starter or the person checking you in at the front desk will tell you which tee colors are normally played by the average man, average woman, superstar man, superstar woman, senior, or junior golfer. Typically, red is for women, gold for senior men, white for men, and blue and black for big hitters.

If you are playing with both men and women at different tees, whoever uses the farthest back tee tees off first. If two couples are playing and the men are playing from one color tee, the honor goes to the best score on the previous hole, between the two men. The one with honors tees off first. The honor at the women's tee goes to the woman with the best score on the previous hole as well. On the first hole, since there are no honors yet, I ask if she would prefer I go first or if she would like to.

Again, it's time to be quiet. As much laughing as my sisters and I do, and as talkative and boisterous as we are, we are always quiet on the tee box. It's a hard-and-fast rule. This means keep everything quiet. No talking, no coughing, no rustling around in your bag, and no opening or closing zippers. Keep your body still, and don't practice swing or stretch when someone else has addressed the ball. (To address the ball means they have acquired their final stance in preparation to hit the ball.) This also means no cell phones ringing. In fact, many golfers are quite offended if you bring your phone on the course. The safe thing is to leave it in the car or, at the very least, turn the sound off. Many private golf courses have very strict cell phone rules. You should check with your host, the pro shop, or the course's website if you have questions.

Where do you stand on the tee when you're not the one hitting the ball? For a right-handed golfer, you should stand so that if she were to look up, you would be in the one to two o'clock range. For safety's sake—and so they don't have to wonder where you are—never stand behind her. She should not have to stop and look to see where you are to make sure she doesn't hit you with the ball or a swinging club.

The rule is: *Never* stand in front of someone's ball. Always stand even with or behind it.

It is very tempting to break this rule, especially when it's mixed men and women. You may be tempted to drive the cart a little further ahead and sit there while the men tee off. *Don't.*

A friend of mine will never be tempted to do this again. She had decided to get some water at the cooler, which was slightly in front of the men's tee. Her husband is a very accomplished golfer and would never shank one off the club sideways . . . at least not on purpose. His ball shot out from the club almost directly sideways, hit his wife on the bicep, and knocked her to the ground. Though it didn't turn out to be tragic, it definitely hurt. Had she been hit somewhere else, it would have been more unpleasant than a bruise on the arm. It will be tempting. Don't do it.

If the sun is low or for some reason the ball is hard to see, help others watch their balls. They may often ask for your help. You should be far enough back that they can't see you in their backswings. You may even want to tell them, "I'm going to stand behind you so I can help watch." If you are hitting into the sun, there is nothing wrong with asking someone else to help watch your ball.

What happens if you swing and miss a tee shot? Sometimes nerves can get the best of me, and it happens. A whiff is a common thing for the novice golfer. Try not to let it rattle you. This is a time to forget about the past and think only of the future. You will notice that professional golfers are very good at this. Tee the ball up again and calmly attempt another tee shot. If you intended to hit the ball, it is a stroke. If your ball falls off the tee by accident while you are doing a practice swing, it is not a stroke.

Once you have hit your ball, keep your eye on it. This is not the time to be angry that it went into the woods. Chances are that when you are angry, you are not watching where the ball goes. In fact, there is never a time to let anger get in the way of the enjoyment of the game. No one wants to play with a bad sport. When having a bad round, I go out of my way to make sure I don't affect the other three players. If I'm disgusted with myself and they can tell or, worse yet, if they have to listen to me complain, I am negatively affecting their game. Now it's not fun anymore. We have all heard the guy a few holes away throw his club into the water. That may be amusing from afar, but I can tell you, the other three people are not enjoying themselves. If I have a bad shot, I might say, "Well, it's always good to have something to work on at the range."

There are two estimates needed to mark where your ball went: line and distance. To track what line your ball was on, pick something in the horizon you can use as a marker. Example: It went straight toward the out-of-bounds white marker or maybe that pine tree. Distance is tough, especially if you are a long hitter.

As I get older, my eyesight is not as sharp, and I am starting to have more of an issue determining distance. Make an effort to notice if your ball has gone farther than that tree you were eying but not as far as the fence post. A rule of thumb for me is that the ball usually does not go as far as I think it does. Good etiquette is not having to ask the others where they think your ball went every time you hit. Occasionally, we all have to ask for help finding a ball, but try not to make it every hole. It's your ball—your responsibility. In fact, make note of where the other balls went so you know who hits next. They will definitely appreciate it if you find their balls when they have lost track of them.

"Do you actually think you hit it this far, or were you just hoping?"

HOLE NUMBER 6

On the Fairway

When is it safe to hit?

On the first tee, it is easy to know when to hit because the starter tells you when you can begin. He or she is watching the group ahead of you and will tell you when it is time to proceed to the first tee.

This is when most players address the ball and practice some sort of pre-shot routine. As a beginner, make sure your routine is fast. Try not to be the player who takes three practice swings before hitting every ball.

It is safe to hit when you are sure that you cannot hit the ball as far as the group playing ahead of you. If you see someone about to hit, and there are people who might be in the way, you might suggest they wait. It is possible the hitter cannot see them.

Keep in mind that there may be golfers from another hole on your hole, not only the ones in front of you. Someone on another hole may have hit a shot off her own fairway onto yours and may walk on to hit her ball.

If you hear someone yell, "Fore," do not look up to see where the ball is or you may end up sporting a black eye—or making a trip to the hospital. Turn your back to where the sound came from, cover the back of your head, and get into a low crouch. If you think your ball may sail toward another golfer and could cause harm, it is definitely appropriate to yell "fore" to alert them.

While hitting on the fairway, if your club takes a chunk out of the grass, which is called a divot, be sure to pick up the chunk of grass, place it back into the hole on the ground, grass side up, and lightly step it down. Some carts also have a container of grass seed or sand you can sprinkle over the divot. This will help speed up regrowth.

After the first shot, play now progresses to whosever ball is farthest from the pin—that is, the hole's flag post. That person hits first. If that person is you, and after hitting two or three times, you are struggling to get the ball down the fairway, you may decide to pick up the ball and drop it about one hundred yards from the green—or to drop it directly on the green. No one cares what *you* decide to do. It's your game. If you want to pick it up, pick it up. Better that than to delay play.

When your ball is ahead of the other players and they are taking their shots, you should be preparing to hit your ball as long as it does not distract them. As soon as the last of them hit, address your ball and hit.

One of my friends told me that if you're not getting paid the big bucks on Sunday afternoon (because you won the tournament), it doesn't hurt to pick up your ball or give yourself an advantage occasionally. My only caution is not to brag about your score at the end if you gave yourself several mulligans or do-overs.

Know which ball is yours and don't *ever* hit someone else's ball. Even if you don't think anyone else is on the entire course, do not hit or pick up another ball. My sisters and I have a little saying now when we find a ball in the middle of nowhere: "Must be Bob's ball." One time, we were golfing on a hot summer day and thought no one was in front of us. We were wrong. Bob was about three holes ahead of us and had hit an errant ball onto the rough of our fairway. He was now looking for his ball. I had assumed it was a ball from the day before, so I had picked it up and kept walking. Up walked Bob. He had been looking and looking for his ball and asked if we had seen it. I didn't know what to do. I was tempted to drop the ball out of my pocket and say, "Here it is," but I didn't. I've never picked up another ball again. I still feel bad for Bob.

"How long should I look for my ball if I lose it?" As I said earlier, my sisters and I play ready-golf. If someone can't find her ball or it takes her a while to get to her ball, and my ball is closer to the pin—meaning that technically, I would not hit next—I will still hit next if we are playing ready-golf. It keeps up the pace of play and makes it less formal. After I hit, I help her find her ball.

The pros have a three-minute rule in looking for a lost ball. I suggest you should spend less. Three minutes is a long time. You might need to nicely encourage a golfer in your foursome to drop the extra ball from her pocket and play that ball instead. If you think you might have a findable ball, do a quick run through the woods or long grass once or twice, as long as your search is not holding anyone up. Any longer than that needs to be saved for the day you are playing in the big tournament.

If your ball goes deep in the woods, drop a ball near where the ball went in, within its line of flight, no closer to the hole. Yes, it counts as a stroke. Example: The ball you hit in the woods, one stroke. The ball you set down, second stroke. Hit the new ball, third stroke.

It is very tempting after you hit your fourth shot into the woods to ask your partners what you're doing wrong. I recommend that you do this sparingly. I can always ask my husband for a little help, and he will often fix what I am doing wrong with a few words. But in general, most people do not go golfing hoping they get paired up with someone who wants a free lesson out of the deal. It's okay to ask occasionally, "Can you see what I'm doing wrong?" And it is possible that they will be able to help, but you are better off saving instructional questions for the driving range, a golf clinic, or a lesson.

When *do* you touch the ball? When *don't* you touch the ball?

Once you have placed the ball on the tee, it is considered "in play." Anything you do to move the ball is a stroke. When playing a relaxed game, like I do with my sisters, we don't care if someone swings and misses the ball; *however*, it is assumed that if you *do not* count it, you are not keeping a "true" score. It is probably not very nice to tout your score to your mates if you are not counting every stroke.

Technically a stroke is when you:

hit the ball;

have intent to hit the ball but miss it (a whiff);

move grass and leaves around the ball to get a cleaner shot, and it inadvertently moves the ball;

pick up your ball on the edge of a swamp and throw it out to a better hitting area. This is not acceptable in professional golf; however, it is often done in casual golf;

kick your ball with your foot because it is underneath a tree branch, commonly known as a "foot wedge"; or

hit the ball into someone's yard. (You should never go into a yard to retrieve a ball and definitely never hit from someone's yard. Count it as a stroke and set a new ball down in bounds.)

If you land on a cart path, in a temporary body of water, or in an area marked "Under Maintenance" or

"Ground Under Repair," you are allowed and required to move your ball outside the hazard, as the course does *not* want you stepping on any hazard area. You must drop your ball within one club-length of the ground under repair, no closer to the hole. This is not considered a stroke or point.

If you hit your ball out of bounds (OB) off the tee, technically, you must count the stroke and hit another tee shot, called a provisional ball. In the event that you find your first ball and it is not OB, you may continue using the first ball and pick up your provisional ball. When I am playing with my sisters, we don't really care much about the score. To keep pace-of-play, we may not bother hitting a provisional tee shot, instead dropping a ball near where we thought it went OB, within the line of flight, and no closer to the hole than it appeared to travel.

The worst offense here is if you are playing by the rules but don't hit a provisional ball, only to find that your tee shot was indeed out of bounds. In this case, you technically have to return to the tee box and hit a new tee shot. This can really wreak havoc on pace-of-play. It's better to hit a provisional tee shot, just in case.

The same is true with any shot that goes out of bounds. Technically, you should return to where you hit the ball from and count it as one stroke. Very few people do this unless they are playing tournament golf.

If your ball lies on a cart path, or if your stance requires you to stand on a cart path, you may take relief without taking a stroke. Move the ball no closer to the hole within one club-length and drop the ball.

The new stroke-and-distance local rule allows players the option of dropping in the fairway if they so choose. Players must find where their ball went out of bounds and draw an imaginary line perpendicular to the fairway, no closer to the hole. From there, they can drop anywhere within two club-lengths behind the line.

If you're just getting started at golf and don't know all the rules, don't beat yourself up. You will learn them over time. No one knows all the rules when they first start. You can always go to the USGA website for all new rules, but here are a few that are good to know:

- You may only have a maximum of fourteen clubs in your bag. There are penalties if you have more than that.

- Put your tee in the ground behind the tee markers. If you accidentally tee off in front of them, it is a two-stroke penalty. You can place your tee up to two club-lengths behind them if you need to find an even lie for your feet.

- Out-of-bounds areas are identified by white steaks in the ground.

- Hitting out of bounds is a two-shot penalty, and you have to replay the previous shot. When you hit a ball out of bounds, you must go back to where you hit the previous shot. Example: if your tee shot is out of bounds, you will re-tee and instead of hitting your second shot, you will hit your third shot.

- If you have hit a shot that you think might be out of bounds, don't wait to get up there to figure it out. Hit a provisional ball by clearly announcing to your foursome what you are doing. This way, you won't have to walk or ride back to the tee to hit a new tee shot since you've already hit a provisional. If you find your first ball, you do not use your provisional shot.

- There are lateral hazards and water hazards, not called penalty areas. I am not going to go into those details in this book. There are many rules about unplayable lies as well. I am not going to go into all the different rules and options. No one will fault you for not knowing them, especially while you are learning the sport.

- Lost Ball Rule: if you do lose a ball, there is a one-shot penalty, and you play it as if it was hit out of bounds. I will point out that this is a time when my sisters and I do not go back to where we hit the previous ball. We just keep playing from where we are at.

- Courses may implement a local rule (not for competition) that offers an alternative to the stroke-and-distance penalty for lost balls or shots hit out of bounds. A player may drop a ball anywhere between where the original ball was believed to come to rest (or went out of bounds) and just into the edge of the fairway, but no nearer the hole. The golfer takes a two-stroke penalty and plays on instead of returning to the tee. This way, the local rule mimics your score if you had played a decent provisional ball.

- Do not ground your club in the sand. If your ball goes in the sand, you must hover over it before hitting it. If you do ground your club, it is a one-stroke penalty.

- If you need to drop your ball—for example, if it was out of bounds—you must drop it from knee height.

HOLE NUMBER 7

Bunkers

Bunkers (also called sand traps) are designed to make the game interesting, challenging, and often frustrating. You have to love them for what they are. I try to have a positive attitude when I land in one. When approaching your ball in the trap, take the shortest route possible so that you have less to rake when finished. I recommend locating the rake before you enter the bunker, taking it with you, and always entering the bunker on the low side rather than the high side when possible. When exiting the bunker, tap your shoes with your club to remove excess sand to prevent tracking it onto the putting surface.

A new rule now allows you to remove loose impediments in the bunker, such as rocks or sticks, but you are still not allowed to "ground" your club before you hit out of a trap. This means that your club cannot sit on or touch the ground while you are preparing for your shot. The club must hover above the ground, not touching the sand or the ball, until you take your shot. Once you have hit it out of the trap, take a rake and smooth out any marks your shoes or the ball have made, leaving it as flat as possible for the golfers behind you.

My goal is to leave the bunker better than I found it. Do not try to simply scrape it over with your shoe. Take the rake provided, and smooth out all your footprints and ball marks. Different courses have different rules about whether the rake should be left in the trap or on the grass surrounding the trap. Just leave it as you found it.

My sisters and I love to remember the course we played in Mexico. They gave each foursome a rake to carry with them for eighteen holes. Try putting one of those in your bag!

HOLE NUMBER 8

Around the Greens

A green is the somewhat circular, short-grass area around the hole and flag. It is important to understand that the turf on the green is very specialized. Great care goes into maintaining it. It is very sensitive and needs to be respected. You should never drive a cart, place your bag, pivot your shoe, or walk with a hard heel on the greens. This will harm them, and it will also change the putting surface for the players behind you by creating bumps and indentations that will make their putting difficult. Even carrying your bag across the green means adding a lot of weight to your step, which is also hard on the greens.

If your ball is off the green or on the fringe, which is the three to six feet of transition grass surrounding the green, the pin or flag stays in the hole. Just recently, a new golf rule was adopted that allows all golfers to leave the pin in at all times. If you would like the pin pulled for your putt, you may pull it or ask one of your mates to pull it for you.

When pulling the pin, try not to jam the end of the pin into the green or drop the flag on the green. Remember, this is very sensitive grass.

If someone's putt is so far away that they can't see the hole, she may ask if someone can "tend" the pin for her. This means that she would like it pulled but is so far away that she needs the pin held gently in the hole until the ball approaches. When tending the pin, pull it out far enough that it is no longer touching anything in the hole, clasp the flag in your hand if it's windy so it doesn't distract, and keep the pin straight in the air. After they hit the ball, pull the pin before the ball approaches the hole.

The rule of thumb is that the person with the ball closest to the hole is the one who pulls the flag because the person whose ball is farthest away is first to putt. With the new rules, adopted in 2019, however, you no longer need to pull the flagstick when putting. This speeds up play.

Once your ball is in the hole, you should remove it as it may cause another ball to bounce out of the hole.

However, if you are playing casual golf, you may leave it in the cup until the others have finished.

Remember that whoever is farthest out hits next. She may actually be putting before someone closer to the pin who needs to chip.

Once again, be quiet when anyone is putting. Very quiet. It is tempting to talk when you are this close to each other. But when someone addresses the ball, it's time to be silent.

If you made a fairly long or hard shot that landed on the green, it probably left a mark. This is called a ball mark or divot, and when you are on the green, it is good practice to fix the indentation made. If you don't have a ball-mark tool, use your tee to fix the ball mark. Most people lift up on the tee too much. This actually pulls the grass roots out. It doesn't work and is not helpful.

A better technique is to "close it up" by pushing the edges of the divot together. To do this, first stick the tee in the ground near the edge of the divot, then with the tee still in the ground, push the tee toward the center of the divot. Do this three or four times, circling the edge of the divot.

How to Fix Your Divots

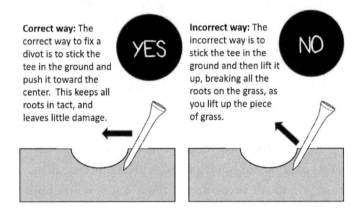

Correct way: The correct way to fix a divot is to stick the tee in the ground and push it toward the center. This keeps all roots in tact, and leaves little damage.

YES

Incorrect way: The incorrect way is to stick the tee in the ground and then lift it up, breaking all the roots on the grass, as you lift up the piece of grass.

NO

You will look very smart if you do it correctly. I have seen very experienced golfers do a poor job of fixing divots. If you want to look really accomplished, fix an extra divot or two. This shows that you definitely know what you are doing and that you appreciate keeping the course in good shape.

Etiquette says that when you arrive on the green, you mark the ball with a marker. Put the mark behind the ball so it does not affect the ball's lie. Some people try to put it under the ball. This is not correct because you are altering your lie.

Now is the time when you may legally touch your ball. You may clean your ball, adjust how it is facing, or even change balls at this time. When I am with my sisters, we do not mark the ball unless it is in someone's way. If a ball appears to be in my way or if its presence is distracting, I will ask, "Would you mind marking your ball?" If in doubt, mark it. When I am golfing with guys from work, it is a given that we mark our balls every time, all the time. The new rules adopted in 2019 also allow you to fix any ball marks in the line of your putt.

Keep your body out of the other golfers' lines of sight, and do not step on or near the lines they are putting, as it causes indentations in the green. A putt's line usually extends twice the distance from the ball to the hole. If someone's ball is ten feet from the cup, you can stand twenty feet behind or in front of her. The line you shouldn't step on extends three feet beyond the hole as well. This is in case they putt long and need to putt back to the hole. Also keep your shadow out of their line as it can be distracting.

I have also been told it is not appropriate to suggest to other players that "it's okay to step on my line." I had thought I was being polite by saying that. I truly hadn't cared as I knew my putting wasn't going to lead to a great score anyway, but my friend told me this sentiment suggested that it was okay for me to step on her line as well. Many serious golfers are not going to appreciate that.

Something else to note is that some courses code whether the hole is placed near the front, middle or back of the green by the color of the flag. The superintendent and his crew change the hole placement regularly to keep wear and tear on the green to a minimum and to make the course continually challenging for those who golf it regularly.

For example, on our course, red means the hole is placed on the front third of the green, white in the middle third, and blue in the back. This will be noted somewhere. Some courses have a system in which all flags are positioned at a number three position for the day. These courses will have a diagram on the cart or scorecard that shows where the flag is placed for each hole for the number three positioning. This is helpful since as you become a better golfer, it is useful to know a more accurate distance to the hole.

The golf superintendent, also known as a greenskeeper or turf manager, is the person who is in charge of the grounds of the entire golf course, which includes all grasses short and long, landscaping, and flowers. This person manages the employees required to keep everything in tip-top shape.

If I were to ask our superintendent what three tips he would like to give all golfers, he would say:

Fix ball marks on the greens.

Repair divots on the fairway.

Don't cut the corners on the cart paths (as this can wear out the grass).

As we discussed earlier, calculate your score, clean your ball, or do whatever else you need to do *at the next hole.* Do not waste time standing at the hole you just completed. This holds up the foursome behind you—and everyone behind them as well.

Gimmes: A "gimmie" is when you pick up the ball without putting it into the cup. If you choose to do so, it still counts as a stroke. It is usually a way of complimenting a teammate on a good putt that didn't quite go in.

But I always think it's rude for someone to say, "That's a gimme," to me when I have a five-foot putt left to make it in the hole. First of all, there is nothing more gratifying than hearing the sound of my ball dropping into the cup. And secondly, I want a true score. I also need to practice making those putts. If my golf-mate gives me an unusually long gimme that I want to putt out, I nicely say, "Thanks, but I think I'm going to putt it out. I need a little work on these."

There is no sure putt. If you watch professional golf, you know this to be true. If it were a sure thing, the professionals would all pick up their balls when they get close to the hole. I prefer to putt everything out. However, if someone is a new golfer or a slow golfer and she's already putted two or three times, it is courteous for her to pick up her ball and move on. Putting back and forth over the hole isn't fun for anyone.

In reality, five-foot putts take as much concentration and focus as thirty-foot putts. Having said this, it is very common for someone to say a two-inch putt is a gimme.

"I never cheat on anything, well except my golf score, and maybe my taxes, or if the sales lady forgets to charge me for something, or if I'm sneaking into the movie theatre, but never anything important."

HOLE NUMBER 9

Your Score

Keep track of your own score. Do not expect your spouse or someone else to keep it for you. Asking, "What did I get on that hole?" is okay once in a while, but don't make a habit of it. They have to keep track of their own scores.

You may choose to keep score or not, as golf is such an individual sport. My sisters tend to celebrate pars, birdies, and nice shots but choose not to keep an overall score.

I do recommend that if you are keeping score, you shouldn't cheat. I have a friend who *never* cheats on her score because she considers everyone she golfs with a prospective client for her business and wants them to trust her. Trust isn't going to come if you cheat on your score. They may wonder what else you cheat on. So beware, others may be judging you. As golfing great P.G. Wodehouse once said, *"To find a man's true character, play golf with him."*

When I was a beginner, I religiously wrote down every whiff. I counted every foot wedge and every stroke, not because it was pleasant for me, but so I could track my improvement.

After golfing with a variety of people, I found that many golfers don't count absolutely everything. Once again, it's your game—you track what you want to track. However, if you're playing for money or competition, you need to count everything.

Some people will miss a putt, pick up their ball, and move on, acting as if they made it. That's fine if you are golfing with friends or don't care about your score. If you are out on the course with people who may be deciding whether they will do business with you or not, I would say, "Looks like I need to work on those," and putt into the cup rather than scoop it up without having actually made the putt.

For the novice golfer, I suggest keeping track of achievements. Write down the number of bogeys, pars, and birdies for each round. Keep a running score of them throughout the year; always trying to improve on your best score. Some people track the number of putts per nine or eighteen holes. Do whatever works for you. You may choose not to keep score at all. That's the beauty of golf. It is an individual sport if you want it to be.

My husband and I will often play a game inside the game that has nothing to do with the score. Look on the internet for golf games. "Bingo, Bango, Bongo" is our favorite. The first point is awarded to the first ball to land on the green. The second point goes to the closest to the pin, once all balls are on the green. The third point goes to the first ball in the cup. This makes the game challenging, more fun, and helps us focus. These games are designed to make it possible for anyone to win, no matter what level.

As you become a more proficient golfer, scoring will definitely get easier, and keeping track of your improvement will become more fun. I always smile when I see the quote by Jeff Sluman, *"I hate this game, and I can't wait to play again tomorrow."*

At the end of the round, it is common courtesy to shake hands with your foursome *on the green* of the last hole and tell them it was a great day of golf. This is not done in the clubhouse or in the parking lot but on the last hole. You will also notice that it is common courtesy for men to remove their caps before shaking hands.

"I got a ten, but put me down for a seven."

AFTER YOUR ROUND

"How Did Your Round Go?"

The typical question the seventeen-year-old cart boy and the guy at the end of the bar are going to ask is, "How did your round go?" The best answer is "Great!" They do not need to hear about your awful round, your drive into the woods, your poison ivy, and the rest. They are making conversation. I used to think I had to score under one hundred before I could tell the cart boy I played a good round. I have now learned that all he really wants to know is if I had a fun time. Always try to have a good time golfing, no matter what the scorecard says.

Speaking of cart boys: Tipping etiquette obviously varies by course. At some courses, golfers may commonly tip $1 to $2 when the cart boy hands off the cart and another $1 to $5 when they greet you at the end, clean your clubs, and send you on your way. At other courses, golfers only tip at the end. Obviously, courses vary. This is an average rule of thumb. If it is an elite course, you will want to tip more.

THE 19TH HOLE

The restaurant at the course is often called the 19th hole. You have successfully completed your fabulous round of golf, and now it is time to celebrate with your friends. My hope is that you now feel confident enough to make golf a larger part of your life. When your boss, work associates, a salesperson, or maybe a new acquaintance asks you to join them on the course, you won't hesitate and will enthusiastically take them up on it.

Say "yes" to golf—and all the opportunities in life it may present!

GLOSSARY OF GOLF TERMS

- *Address the Ball*: The golfer has addressed the ball when he or she has grounded the club directly behind the ball.

- *Am I Out*: An expression used to ask whether your putt is farthest from the hole and if it is indeed your turn to putt.

- *Apron*: The section immediately around the green where the grass is cut slightly higher than the green and lower than the fairway or the rough.

- *Backswing*: The motion of bringing the club back and away from the ball. The top of the backswing is the point at which a golfer's club reaches the top of the swing. No two are the same. It is important to know that there is no hard-and-fast rule as to how far back you should bring the club. Even the pros are all different.

- *Ball Washers*: They are near some tee boxes. Feel free to use them, but not when someone is addressing the ball, as it is distracting.

- *Birdie*: One stroke under par on a hole. If par is four, then a birdie would be three.

- *Bogey*: One stroke over par on a hole. If par is four, then a bogey would be five. "Bogey golf" means that someone usually scores an average of one over on each hole.

- *Breakfast Ball*: If someone hits a very bad shot on the drive of Hole Number One, they might say, "I'm taking a breakfast ball." This means they are taking a mulligan. For some reason, only a mulligan on Hole Number One is called a breakfast ball. Obviously, this is not an official golf term and should not be used if you are in a tournament or playing a serious game. When playing with my sisters, it is just fine. I have friends who "purposely" take breakfast balls on their first shots when they are playing with someone who is very nervous about not being "a good enough golfer" in order to help put that golfer at ease.

- *Bump and Run*: A pitch shot around the green, intended to hit into the slope, to deaden the speed, before landing on the green and rolling toward the cup.

- *Bunker*: An area on the course filled with sand that exists as a hazard or obstacle. When hitting a shot out of a sand bunker, the rule is that you are not able to "ground" the club first, which means the club cannot touch the ground or rest on the ground before hitting the ball. When finished hitting out of the bunker, it is the golfer or caddy's job to rake the area disturbed by play.

- *Caddy*: A person hired to carry your clubs and provide assistance on which club to use, distances, where to aim, or other aspects of the game based on how the course plays. It is almost required if you are going to take up golf that you watch the movie *Caddyshack*. Few courses have caddies these days. Most people use golf watches, scopes, or apps to help with approximating distances.

- *Cart*: A cart can vary from a personal cart customized like a Porsche to a cart provided by the course or a pull cart that holds your clubs. Some courses use Segways, and a few even have llamas to carry the clubs. Just remember that golf carts are basically small cars; not paying attention or driving them too fast can cause serious injuries to yourself or others.

- *Chip and Run*: A shot played close to the green in which the ball stays low and spends more time on the ground than in the air.
- *Cleaning Your Ball*: It is okay to clean your ball when you're taking relief from an immovable obstruction. You can mark, lift, and clean a ball on the green, but it's a violation to do so when another ball is in motion, as your ball might influence the outcome of that stroke. Cleaning a ball at an inappropriate time is a one-stroke penalty.
- *Club*: Head, hosel, and shaft.
- *Clubface*: The part of the club that strikes the ball.
- *The Cup*: The holy grail. This is the goal of each hole—to hit the ball into the cup.
- *The Dance Floor*: Slang term for the green. "I'm on the dance floor" would be an expression for when your ball lands on the green.
- *Divot*: A piece of turf that has been removed from the ground along with the ball or the hole left in the turf after the shot has been taken.
- *Dogleg Right or Dogleg Left*: A Golf hole that is crooked like the hind leg of a dog.
- *Double Bogey*: Two points over par on a hole. If par is four, then a double bogey would be six.

- *Double Eagle*: Three under par on a hole. If par is five, a double eagle would be two. Needless to say, double eagles are very rare.

- *Draw*: For a right-handed player, this is a shot that flies slightly right to left.

- *Drive*: The tee shot. It is a long shot played from the tee box, usually off a tee.

- *Driver*: The 1-wood, usually the largest club in your bag, intended to go the farthest.

- *Driving Range / Practice Range / Golf Range*: An area where golfers can practice. Commonly you purchase a bucket of balls or a coin to insert in a machine for balls. Often, there are flags or objects you may use for aim. There may be a large green for putting practice.

- *Eagle:* A score of two under par on a hole. If par is five, an eagle would be three.

- *Fade*: For a right-handed player, a shot that flies slightly left to right.

- *Fairway*: The short grass between the tee and the green.

- *Flag*: Identifies the hole or cup where you will putt the ball. Flags are often different colors symbolizing their placement on the green. Example: Red—closest to the front of the green; White—middle of the green; Blue—closest to the back of the green.

- *Fluffy Lie*: When the ball rests on top of long grass.

- *Follow-through*: The part of the swing that happens after the ball has been struck.
- *Fringe*: The three to six feet of transition grass surrounding the green.
- *Grip*: How you grip the club. This has a very large influence on how you hit the ball.
- *Greens*: Where the flag and hole are located. They are very delicate grasses.
- *Handicap*: A number that measures a golfer's potential, used to make it possible for golfers of varying abilities to compete against one another.
- *Hazard*: Water hazards and man-made hazards such as bunkers or sand traps make the course more interesting and difficult.
- *Hole in One*: When the tee shot goes directly in the hole, your score is one. These are very rare, and sometimes, it is expected that if you get a hole in one, you will buy the other golfers in the clubhouse a round of drinks. Sam Snead, a famous PGA golfer, is known for forty-two hole in ones. The most amazing thing is that he has made a hole in one using every club in his bag, except the putter.
- *Hook*: For a right-handed player, a shot that curves sharply right to left.

- *Honors*: Whoever had the lowest score on the previous hole is honored by teeing off first on the next hole.

- *Hosel*: The area on a club where the head fits into the shaft.

- *Hybrids*: Golf clubs that tend to be part wood and part iron.

- *Impact*: The moment when the club hits the ball.

- *Intended Line of Flight*: The flight that the player was intending the ball to take.

- *Irons*: These are the iron clubs in your set. Often included are a sand wedge (used to hit out of the sand or some short shots), a pitching wedge, and a lob wedge (used for your shortest shots), as well as a 3-, 4-, 5-, 6-, 7-, 8- and 9-iron. Irons are generally used for shorter distances, whereas woods are used for longer distances.

- *Layup Shot*: Made from the fairway after the drive, when because of a hazard, the golfer chooses to make a shorter shot than usual or a more accurate shot.

- *Lob Shot*: A short but high shot attempting to land softly on the green without roll; often hit with a wedge.

- *Lob Wedge*: A club specifically designed to hit the ball short yet high, with the intent of landing without roll.

- *Loft*: The degree of the angle on the clubface. A club with a high loft (a wedge or 9-iron) should hit the ball high in the air, while a lower loft (a 3- or 4-iron) should hit the ball farther and less high.

- *Lie*: Where the ball sits after it stops moving from a shot.

- *Mulligan*: When a golfer takes a second shot from a tee without counting his or her first shot. This is technically not allowed and usually occurs when the golfer is unhappy with the first shot. It is common to have the opportunity to "buy a mulligan" at a charity event. Some players will call the first-hole mulligan a *breakfast ball*.

- *Out of Bounds (OB)*: Considered "off the course" and typically marked by white steaks in the ground. Officially, if the ball is hit OB, the player must take a two-stroke penalty and hit from the point where the previous ball was hit. A provisional ball may be hit if a golfer's ball is suspected to be OB. When playing with friends, one might choose not to go all the way back to the tee box in the event the drive is OB.

- *Pace-of-Play*: The pace at which one or more golfers plays through a round. Many courses will post an average pace-of-play time and encourage players to stay within that timeframe. A ranger or official may be riding the course on a golf cart encouraging slow foursomes to speed up or pick up their pace of play.

- *Par*: The score established by the golf club for each hole that an accomplished player should get. For example, on a par-four a player would hit a drive, a fairway shot, an approach shot, and one putt. A par golfer is someone who usually scores exact par or an average of par on each hole.

- *The Pin*: The flag or marker for the hole. It may be removed when all players are on the green, then returned to the hole after everyone has completed their putt. With the new rules, it does not have to be removed at all.

- *Pitch and Run*: A shot intended to fly a short distance, then run on the ground.

- *Pitch Shot*: A shot that spends more time in the air than on the ground. These tend to be further from the green than a chip shot and therefore require longer swings.

- *Players Assistant*: Sometimes called a *ranger* or *official*. They provide assistance to golfers and help maintain pace-of-play.

- *Pre-shot Routine*: The purpose of this ritual is to get the player into the proper mindset to hit the ball. Many golfers have a ritual they follow before every single shot.

- *Provisional Ball*: If a player believes that his or her first shot may have gone out of bounds (OB), a provisional ball may be hit that is used only in the event that the first ball is OB. Under the new USGA rules, a golfer can choose to hit another ball from the tee with a one-stroke penalty *or* they may proceed to where the ball crossed the OB line, drop a ball, and take a two-stroke penalty.

- *Putt*: When a player uses their putter to roll the ball across the green in hopes of landing in the hole. Golfers often keep track of putts with the goal being two putts or less per hole.

- *Ranger*: A ranger oversees the play, ensuring that the golfers maintain the rules and practice etiquette.

- *Reading the Green*: The part of course-management wherein the player attempts to determine which way a putt will curve and how fast it might travel on any green.

- *The Rough*: The area of the fairway that has been left more natural. It usually contains longer grasses that make play more difficult when hit into the rough.

- *Sand Trap*: An area of sand in the fairway or around the greens created for interest and difficulty.

- *Scorecard*: Each course has its own scorecard. At the very least, it will contain what is considered par for each hole. It may include pictures of the fairways with short explanations of holes, information on hole placement, or yardages to hazards.

- *Scramble*: A game often played in a tournament or fundraiser in which each player hits a shot and then the foursome progresses down the fairway using whichever of the four shots is the best.

- *Shank*: When the ball is hit, usually with an iron, without connecting solidly with the clubhead. For example, striking the ball on the hosel.

- *Short Game*: Shots played on or around the green, including pitch shots, chips, and putts.

- *Shotgun*: When players in a tournament begin playing at the same time on different holes, commonly signaled to begin with a gunshot, or more commonly a horn, that can be heard throughout the course.

- *Slice*: For a right-handed golfer, a ball that severely curves from left to right.

- *Stance*: The position of a player's feet when addressing the ball. A closed stance means that the feet are very close, while an open stance means that they are farther apart.

- *Stroke*: A stroke is one shot or one point.

- *Superintendent*: Formally called the greenskeeper. The person who professionally manages the labor as well as the seed, fertilizer, water, and other materials needed to keep the course in excellent shape.

- *Take a Drop*: Typically taken after hitting the ball into an area from which a player cannot or chooses not to play the next shot. If the ball is out of bounds, the player receives a penalty stroke for taking a drop. A penalty stroke is not taken if the drop is done due to interference or course condition.

- *Tee*: The plastic or wood object used to hold your ball in the air so you may hit it. Some are long, some short. It is personal preference. You are only allowed to use a tee on the tee box that is designated for your first shot of each hole. You may never use a tee anywhere else on the course, unless using it to fix ball marks on the green.

- *Tee Box*: This is the raised landmass at the start of each hole where you tee off. Teeing off is hitting the ball off the tee. The tee box may simply be referred to as the *tee*. When placing your tee and ball in the ground, you must be behind the tee markers. If not, it is a two-stroke penalty.

- *Tee Time*: The actual time that is reserved to hit your first ball. Therefore, you should be at the tee box at least five minutes early. Different courses have different time allowances for each hole. It is usually published online how long a round of eighteen holes will take on a course.

- *Tee-Marker Colors*: These are markers on each tee box set at varying distances. The golfer may choose from which color they will tee off for the entire round. There are forward tees and back tees. Usually, a golfer will choose which tee to use based on the length of his or her average drive.. Leagues, charity events, and tournaments will tell you which tee you must use.

- *The Turn*: This designates the time between the ninth and tenth hole. It means you are halfway done with your eighteen holes. There is often a restroom as well as snacks and beverages. The course allows the same amount of time for the turn as the time to play one hole. If they allow seven minutes per hole, they allow seven minutes at the turn. It is not meant to be a sit-down lunch. Traditionally, this is a time when golfers grab a hot dog, a snack, or a beverage—on the run.

- *Waggle*: Motion a player may make while addressing the ball, designed to relax them and help their swing.

- *Whiff*: When you attempt to hit the ball but miss it entirely. Also known as an airball. This technically counts as a stroke.

- *Woods*: These are the large-headed clubs in your set. In the past, they were always made of wood. Now, they are made from enhanced materials such as graphite, titanium, or kevlar. The 1-wood is called the driver. It is the largest and is used to hit the ball the farthest. There are often 3-, 5- and 7-woods in most golfers' bags. Woods are generally used for longer distances, whereas irons are used for shorter distances.

- *Nine or Eighteen Holes*: A regulation golf course is made up of eighteen holes. Obviously, playing nine holes takes less time, so that is an option. The front nine is Holes 1 through 9, and the back nine is Holes 10 through 18. The total length of the course, depending on which color tees you are using, will be noted on the scorecard.

- *Yips*: A temporary condition, possibly caused by mental stress, when a player is unable to control a certain club—most commonly the putter.

ELEVEN REASONS WHY YOU SHOULD PLAY GOLF

1. It's good for your health and your cardiovascular system, not to mention flexibility. Without even realizing it, you are getting wonderful exercise. If you walk eighteen holes of golf, you will have taken approximately twelve-thousand steps.
2. It has been shown to reduce stress.
3. It's a great way to make new friends who all have something in common.
4. People will include you in office outings, fundraisers, and family fun that you might miss if you don't golf.

5. You get to enjoy being outdoors, listening to birds and appreciating all the nature around you.
6. You may improve business relationships because four hours with someone allows you to get to know that person personally as well as professionally.
7. There will be many opportunities to network with people you would like to get to know.
8. You may meet potential new clients who need another person in their foursome or are golfing alone on a business trip.
9. It's a great way to challenge yourself. It can be very fulfilling to see improvement.
10. Thanks to handicaps, golfers of all abilities can compete against one another on a level playing field.
11. It is a great reason to travel to fun and interesting places.